Leaves By Night,

Flowers By Day

The 2006 Iowa Poetry Source

Edited by

Rustin Larson, Nynke Passi, and Christine Schrum

1st WORLD
PUBLISHING

Leaves By Night, Flowers By Day

Edited By

Rustin Larson, Nynke Passi, and Christine Schrum

© 2006 1stWorld Publishing

Published by 1stWorld Publishing
1100 North 4th St. Fairfield, Iowa 52556
tel: 641-209-5000 • fax: 641-209-3001
web: www.1stworldpublishing.com

First Edition

LCCN: 2006907340
SoftCover ISBN: 978-1-59540-874-7
HardCover ISBN: 978-1-59540-873-0
eBook ISBN: 978-1-59540-875-4

Cover artwork by Geoffrey Baker

Praise for *Leaves by Night, Flowers by Day*

"Leave your preconceived notions at home; though this journey may begin in Iowa, there is nothing corn-fed or laconic about these poems. This book is so lushly and unabashedly lyrical, so consistently infused with spirit, it nearly levitates. Even the most traditional subjects are imbued with uncommon grace and a touch of exoticism. The editors have done a terrific job with organization, too. Reading through, I couldn't help but imagine all these poets in the same room, an extended family feeding off each other's energy; the flow is that organic and smooth."

—Mark, Cox, author of *Natural Causes*

"*Leaves by Night, Flowers by Day*, filled with unusually compelling visions of revealed beauty, here and as far away as Asia, will keep you awake by kerosene light, or riveted to the page while you take your leisure under the jasmine blossoms of our moment."

—Roger Weingarten, author of *Premature Elegy by Firelight*

"The editors of *Leaves by Night* have created a unique gift for us by their careful selections of poetry from Diane Frank, W.E. Butts, and Michael Carrino, to name just a few. Poetry is the possibility of language and with this book, as Dianna Henning might say, they are spanning the empty space with possibility."

—Dan Troxell, host of Poetry at Zanzibar's

"Leaves by Night, Flowers by Day is a stunning collection of poetry with every page providing surprise and insight. This is a book to read and reread, to carry with you by day and by night."

—Mary Swander, author of
The Desert Pilgrim: En Route to Mysticism and Miracles

"When I went over the review copy of *Leaves by Night, Flowers by Day*, I went a little nuts. I hadn't realized that there were so many unique and arresting voices out there. Among the contributing poets I saw some names I knew. I've interviewed a couple of them on my TV show, The Poets' Corner. Needless to say, lovers of modern-day literature will luxuriate among this panoply of poets."

—John Birkbeck, producer and host of *The Poets' Corner*

Acknowledgments

The editors extend grateful acknowledgment to the following publications where the authors' poems first appeared.

Jill Barnet: "Giraffa Camelopardalis" was first published in *North American Review*.

Elinor Benedict: "Celestial Navigation," *Indiana Review*; "A Daughter-in-Law Watches the Old Man Hesitate," *The Tree Between Us* (March Street Press, 1997); "Two Women Leaving Beijing," "*All That Divides Us*" (Utah State Univ. Press, 2000).

W. E. Butts: "Clay Street" and "Sunday Factory" first appeared in *Sunday Factory*, a chapbook from Finishing Line Press (2006).

Michael Carrino: "Lilacs" first appeared in *Poetry Miscellany*. "Potter's Field" first appeared in *Slant*. "Café Sonata" first appeared in *Twisted Roots*.

Diane Frank: "My Mother's Daughter" was previously published in *The Briar Cliff Review*. "They Thought it Was a Dragon Kite" was previously published in *The Haight Ashbury Literary Journal*, and all of these poems are published in *Entering the Word Temple: Poems by Diane Frank*.

Foreword

Dear Readers,

In its inaugural year, the quality and quantity of submissions to the Iowa Source 2006 Poetry Contest more than surpassed our expectations. We were flooded with submissions from local writers—from Fairfield, Iowa City, Cedar Rapids, Sigourney, and other Iowa cities—as well as from states across the country including California, Vermont, Michigan, and New Hampshire, and countries as far away as Australia and Indonesia.

After many months spent poring over manuscripts, we are pleased to present the winners of our 2006 poetry anthology contest. We are certain you will enjoy these poems as much as we did.

Sincerely,

Editors Rustin Larson, Nynke Passi, and Christine Schrum, with Claudia Petrick, Editor of *The Iowa Source*.

Table of Contents

Man Painted Gold

—*Kim Alvarez*

Today, in Rangoon, a man has painted himself
Entirely in gold. It flakes from his skin,
Which is stretching and cracking.
He is smoking four cigarettes at the same time.
Perhaps being God is just too difficult.
Smoke closes his eyes. We cannot see what he is thinking.
I am wrong. He is not thinking. He is dead.
Only bones in gold dust.

Giraffa Camelopardalis

—Jillian Barnet

The first time my husband kissed me, he didn't bend,
he spread his legs, the way a giraffe does when it eats from acacia trees
that are shorter than it is. That's what the kiss felt like:
a taking in, getting of nourishment. At birth, baby giraffes fall
a long way from their mothers—a cruel
entrance into the world. I feel that way sometimes: taken
far from my mother to live with strangers who
were not *of* me—this was not what I was expecting.
I expected her arms
right away and always.
There are studies: a baby can recognize a photo of her mother even if
she has never seen her.
A baby giraffe follows its mother within
two hours of its birth. My husband
is indulgent when I sniff him
when he comes home from work. He says he finds it odd
that I greet him the way animals do. I can tell
what kind of day he's had: sharp and peppery—stressed;
mild and musky—he laughed a lot and was among friends.
My husband believes it's because I never got
to smell my real family; the others
didn't smell right to me.

Some people think
giraffes don't have voice sounds, but the fact is they moan;
they clean their young with long black tongues, as if they could eat them,
as if they love them that much.

Celestial Navigation

—*Elinor Benedict*

In Zanzibar my husband and I climb
　　to a rooftop café, breathing the blue heat
　　　　my mother at home warned would swaddle us
　　　　　　like the veils of dark women gliding through

the ancient *casbah* below. From white minarets
　　sunset's eerie call to prayer floats over us,
　　　　then settles to a hush as loose-winged sailboats
　　　　　　flutter into the harbor like black butterflies. Soon

the clink and chatter of the dinner hour
　　surround us like wind chimes, mingling
　　　　murmurs of Arabic and Swahili with odors
　　　　　　of olive oil, eggplant, Nile perch. Charmed

but uneasy, we squint into twilight to find
　　the comforting steeple of the only church
　　　　in this city's decaying Stone Town. We feel
　　　　　　like a couple of strays from the temperate zone,

sniffing the air for traces of the island's
　　sweet cloves mixed with the sour smell

of a slave trade still flourishing in secret
      the year my mother was born. Thinking

of her alone in the nursing home, waiting
      to tease me again for traveling to Africa
            when I could *just go to a zoo*, I look
                  into darkness at two strange lights

hovering together as if from a silent airship
      searching for someone lost. My hair roots
            tingle as I reach for my husband's sleeve.
                  Next morning in the flicker of satellite

television we learn how we witnessed
      Venus and Jupiter coinciding precisely,
            only such meeting in two thousand years.
                  That afternoon we nap with spices on our breath

when a bellboy knocks, whisks a white message
      under our door. The blurred type reads, *Last night
            your mother died peacefully. She told the nurse
                  about meeting your father, prayed for you,*

then fell asleep. . . . I crumple the paper. Only
      a few days ago I kissed her cheek and touched
            my dead father's smile in the photograph she slept
                  near. When I stood at the door, she made a droll face

and said she'd pray for me *in darkest Africa.*
 How I laughed at her joke, her fear. But after
  last night's heavenly voyage, so unlike the way
   she flailed her fists in air like a child playing

astronaut when she dreamed herself free, driving
 her Oldsmobile again, I close my eyes tight
  and summon a new vision of Mother, fearless
   at the wheel, sailing her bright planet to his.

A Daughter-in-Law Watches
the Old Man Hesitate

—Elinor Benedict

From the kitchen window I watch Grandfather
outside, standing on top of the long wooden
stairway that leads to the lake. Bundled
in blue wool, zipped up for zero, he waits
for something to happen. But what on a day
like this, frozen from thistle to oak,
could the old man expect? Something

about the turn of his head, his leather cap's
earflaps lifted like wings, tells me
he's listening to ice. I know the sound
from another December, the day I stood
on the stairs myself, watching the birches
lean on each other, brittle, ready to drop
their branches on snow. I'd thought then:
old bones breaking. But to Grandfather

it's probably a noise I wouldn't imagine:
Artillery. Blasting in quarries. Hunters
blamming their rifles. Woodcutters felling
the last of the white pines. Or if his mood

is milder, maybe a beaver slapping his tail
on water, or a grouse drumming his wings
for a mate. Whatever the old man thinks,

if he really goes down to the lake, he'll
hear the creak of his elbows reaming out
inches of ice with an auger; knees, knotted
and stiff, snapping with weight as he bends
to the hole with his bucket and gear.

I look him over—bandaged, almost,
in coats and muffler, surely unable to lift
a struggling pike through a small, dark "o."
He hesitates, seems to forget where he is.
If he were an Eskimo woman, they'd send him
off on a floe. But just as I watch him drift out

to sea, he lowers his earflaps, buckles his boots,
and booms down the steps one more time.

Two Women Leaving Beijing

—Elinor Benedict

We follow the evening tide that pulls
us through the railway station's
halls like seawater sucked
into caves. Dazed by the swell,
I see myself among swarms
of fish—one small neon among
swirls of dark silver. They flow

around me like chains, hauling
their burdens from earth's center
where almost everything sleeps.
We inch toward a stairwell, ooze
through its narrows, fan out wide
to a bay where black trains
fume and sigh. At last we grow

legs, walk upright, breathe.
I notice a woman hurrying beside me
the shape of my mother, dangling
a carp in mesh, its body frozen
in weather. I start to live

in her clothes. My son,
his wife and two little ones
shiver in our upstairs room,
anxious to see me thaw out
the prize, stir a white batter,
heat up the stove—but I can't

finish this scene without seeing
my own son, tall, his jaw bearded,
his blue eyes keen, grinning
beside his car with a salmon
hooked on his thumb. Just then

the woman stops, swings her fish
up the steps of the train as I pass
on to mine. She hesitates as if
I had called her and turns
at the door. We look

toward each other like migrant
women of two different tribes,
tending separate fires, clutching
our skins around us, rising to see
who comes.

Red Jack

—*W. E. Butts*

I was twelve that day Father brought me to the home
of his friend, a man living alone, small pension
and afternoons at the window. I remember the percolator's
aroma and dance, a cigar's blue smoke. They sat at the kitchen
table and spoke for a while about the factory closed,
the railroad gone, men they had known lost in the War,
and before that, the Depression and the ten dollar bill
my father left once in his mailbox. And so a boy learned
the tone and gesture of trust and resolve. At my father's wake
seven years later, Red Jack's nephew James stood next to me,
his uncle dead, and we held the silence between us
like a handshake. Once, we had been altar boys,
and served Mass for a priest who kept raising his cup
to the wine cruet, demanding more of Christ's blood,
and when James hid in the sacristy and drank from the rest
until he was sick, I never told. After the funeral, I left town
for college and the decades of mistakes a man can make,
whether he goes away from the place he was born, or not.
James went to work at a local plant, where he lost
two fingers trying to cut metal under a blade
like the older machinists, without using a safety guard.
It was piecework, and he needed the extra money

for the pregnant girlfriend he'd been dating since high school.
They married and, when their two kids had grown
and moved on, divorced. He and I still talk, and last night,
on the phone, it was as if the years of failure, faith, confession,
and hope were being emptied into this single moment,
each of us hanging on to the end of the other's line
and the chance to save ourselves, yet again.

Clay Street

—*W. E. Butts*

Here is the street in summer
and the old elm shadowing the house.
At the corner, the home
of a prosperous automobile dealer,
father to my best friend Charles,
who later became a cop in the city
we all swore to move to someday.
But just now it almost seemed enough
for us boys to count and name the cars
driving toward the Thruway entrance
at the edge of town, or chase each other
past the overgrown field to the creekbank
and grab sunfish shimmering just beneath
the surface of the shallow, murky water.
Or sometimes the village hall fire alarm
would blare, and if it was evening,
the grocer who lived next door
would rush out to join the volunteers.
Then there were the occasional parades:
beauty queens and fireworks, marching bands
and a soldier returning. Midday, the factory
whistles blew, and men and women filled

the dining car downtown. And maybe
we would leave whoever's front porch
we were gathered on to go and watch
the policeman, sales clerk, garage mechanic,
tool-and-die maker, teacher, mayor, and mailman
hunched over the counter, placing orders
with the waitress with piled-up hair,
who knew them all by name and would,
they were certain, deliver them
their plates of guaranteed homecooking.
Some afternoons, Sammy the junkman
came riding by, his old horse pulling
a cart full of metal scraps and cloth,
and when he cried "rags,"
we'd shout back our senseless taunts,
until he neared the small stone bridge
and the house where two spinster sisters lived
with their bachelor brother who never spoke.
Under that bridge we plotted our futures
of high scores and smiling girls, the secret lives
we believed we would have, and called out
then to the echoing shade.

Sunday Factory

—*W. E. Butts*

We walk the long street
Sunday afternoon,
past the stone church, on our way
to visit his place of work.
This is the religion of father and son,
the faith of a boy who's only five,
the factory a blessing of meat and bread,
the big machines still as statues,
an assembly of clocks
to mark the next week's labor.
Here are the instruments of the makers,
their testaments of gears and wheels.
This is where men and women are called
to the daily stations of common task,
and so I stand with my father
in a child's reverent silence.
Tomorrow, he'll enter the loud,
humming chorus of his eight hour shift
to hose down the conveyor belts
so many times his forearms will ache
until they become light as air.
This is when he thinks of the boy

and his schoolbooks, remembers his wife
and her lilac corsage that morning they married.
And he makes what he can from each of these hours
that will, at last, take him home.

Saved

—*W. E. Butts*

My father dealt antiques,
an avocation those times he wasn't
at his factory shift or teaching me,
his only son, some necessary skill
of boyhood—fingers on the seam
of a baseball, earthworm on the hook,
the knife blade slicing away
from my apprenticed hand that gripped
the beginning of something truly made.

People said he had a kind of knack
for recognizing the real value
in the obscure, the worth of wood
beneath aged, peeling paint, the possible
mechanics of those things broken.
And sometimes he'd bring me to that place
of auctioneer's chant and distant past,
mystery of language and the highest bid.

This is where I learned men and women
came to live by code and signal, how
a certain gesture was a promise given,

and wondered who would sit again
at the roll-top desk to turn on the student lamp.
Was there a woman to work the spinning wheel?
Who would gather now at the oak table
to share supper and the day's events?

And when Father and I returned
home with all he could bargain for that day,
there'd be a collection of used books
for me to choose from—Alexandre Dumas,
Zane Gray, Sherlock Holmes, a dime novel—
some adventure that would take a boy
to bed with a flashlight to read
through the late hours under the covers.

Journal

—*W.E. Butts*

On a train to Chicago,
I stayed awake
all night in the club car.
I was seventeen,
enlisted in the Navy,
and knew nothing yet
of Cuba, Castro,
the C.I.A., or Vietnam.

When I returned to my village,
the factory had gone
on to Delaware,
the rail station closed,
but men still lived
under the bridge
by the crossing.
I knew I must leave.

In New York City,
I found work
as a foot messenger,
delivering packages

to elegant brownstones
in upper Manhattan.
I kept a journal,
and recorded my encounters
with professional dogwalkers.

I rode the Amtrak
to Boston,
where I was hired
by Harvard
to transcribe the poems
of Emily Dickinson,
and became dedicated
to the proper placement
of dashes.

Evenings, I walked
past the fishmarket
to the harbor
and its departing ships,
the stone and glass shadows
of the city behind me.
I was at that edge where
what happened next
would be the rest of my life,
or fog shrouding the shoreline.
But there was a woman

I met and sometimes,
late at night, in the dark,
I'd rise from our bed
and go quietly down
the stairs to sit at the table
with paper and pen,
those words that saved me
before emerging again,
under the lamplight.

Café Sonata

—*Michael Carrino*

Lingering over Caffé Toscana
Lorissa must have recalled
a dream: one lost angel,
bent under the weight of bliss,
collapsed inside her pulse.

Desperate for another
liquid sunset, she chose a narrow
footpath down to Lake Champlain;
gazed at red-stained
Vermont hills.

Lorissa once told me, "I'm encircled
by absence; confused
by even believable
truth." I don't know

why, that night,
after one last espresso, she chose
incandescence—brilliant, white
silence, or how that confused angel

must have pleaded for rest,
folded soiled, white wings
over a face Lorissa could not see.

Summer ends
today. I'm alone
under Café Sonata's canopy.

One more espresso-Mocca Con Panna,
then down to Lake Champlain
where I'm going to breathe, inhale
September's burnt ash perfume;

hum melodies, old ballads
recalling trouble and desire.
Such music might appease

any exhausted angel
disoriented in the fire-tempered sky.

Lilacs

—*Michael Carrino*

On a cobbled Montreal street
an old man pushes a wagon
covered by a parasol—sells lilacs

wrapped in white tissue.
He gives you a bouquet
of the deepest lavender; its perfume

heightens the air around you.
Hearing a freighter's horn on the St. Lawrence
you turn to the sunset,

shade your eyes to watch someone
walking toward you, who by his appearance
might be me. Knowing

how quickly longing unwinds darkness, grows
brittle with each moment of absence,
you lean against the old man's sleeve

refusing to disturb this rehearsal.

Potter's Field

—*Michael Carrino*

Those who inspire no memory
escape notice when exposure or disease
overwhelm them. Unclaimed and unidentified,
New York City's dead are borne
to a county morgue. In Manhattan
it's Bellevue:"Where death delights
to aid the living." Untouchable, the homeless
cluster under bridges, burrow
in subway tunnels, escape
suicide, accident, and homicide,
yet, still die natural as a breath;
easy as the living yawn, quivering for a breath.

If the bodies are not decomposed, they are held
for two weeks—few cities take such trouble—
then ferried from the end of Fordham Street
to Hart's Island, an expanse of meadow and lawn,
thickets of oak and chestnut that obscure
a few decrepit shacks, remains
of forgotten good intention—hospitals
for the insane and yellow fever victims,
workhouses for addicts and destitute women.

A memorial's engraved
with two crosses, two open books inscribed
"alpha" and "omega." Inmates
bury the dead. Light duty on a fair day.
There's a lane of willow, a narrow
plot of wildflowers—aster and yarrow.
Near the ferry slip a dinghy,
half-submerged in the shallow water's muck,
is dappled by the white dung of gulls
that circle in the endless sky, glide down
and drop clam shells over rock exposed by low tide,
where cormorants sun themselves—wings outstretched.

The Imaginary Girl

—Suzanne Cody

The imaginary girl
resembles a Greek myth
rejects the dominant paradigm
has bigger fish to fry

The imaginary girl
prefers pink lipstick
is immune to nostalgia
performs minor brain surgery
upon request

The imaginary girl
perpetually involves herself
in theological disputation
spits on the existence of god
is waiting for a train

The imaginary girl
coddles obsessions
peddles unscrupulous lies
grows spare limbs at will

The imaginary girl
looks naked even
when clothed
dances on the Sabbath
persists in changing
the color of her eyes

The imaginary girl
insists on questioning the
veracity of your truth
loses track of time
wears ridiculous shoes

Going Down to Little Egypt

—*Caree Connet*

Minnie Hazeltine Turner Hawkins (Powers)

They say Aunt Mae was born with the veil
and I've always had the sight.
Once, when I was just a little thing, I said,
"That big black bull's agoin' to gore me."
Scared my folks so bad, we moved to town.

I don't know who my real daddy was.
Pap Hawkins took me in when he married Mama.
His first wife died with the last baby.

I was seventeen when I first saw Angus Frick,
standing outside Lowenberg's Dry Goods,
smoking a Meerschaum pipe, orange
as beaver's teeth. He had buck's eyes
and skin the color of cured tobacco.
His father, he said, preached to the Blackfeet.
They called him Raven and gave him
the chief's daughter.

I dimpled and asked Angus to show me
how he loaded his pipe.
In the sawdust under a pumpkin moon,
with Papa's axe glinting in the chopping block,
he thrust his way under my petticoats.

In the back of the family Bible I wrote
Esther Jane Hawkins was born
the 14th Day of July 1893.

Angus being a man with a family,
Papa got Harry Powers to marry me
by getting him a job at the brick factory.
His first wife died after her appendix burst.
Harry died of grief one month
after I went looking for Angus
behind the veil.

Esther Jane Turner Hawkins Powers (Craver)

I first laid eyes on John at the County Fair,
wearing a jaunty hat and smoking a cigar.
I winked. When he didn't follow me,
I went round and winked again.
John quit school after sixth grade to lay brick,

after his mama died of the diphtheria.
That was Laura Belle Dula, don't you know,
the one whose father went to California
in the Gold Rush and was never heard of.

When the Great War come,
John talked about joining up.
I had a hard fit, I was so afraid of losing him.
On the marriage certificate I signed my name
Esther Jane Powers. Then I tore the record page
out of the back of the family Bible.

In them days you couldn't stay in nursing school
if you was married, or a teacher. I went ahead
and studied on my own. And then I took the train
up to Chicago and passed the exam.
That's how we got through the Great Depression
when there warn't much call for brick laying.
I helped the doctor deliver babies,
and come Fair time, I'd dress up as a gypsy
and for a dollar or two—that was a lot of money
in them days—I'd read palms or tea leaves or cards.
I quit telling fortunes the day a woman asked
if she oughta kill her husband.

That's me with all them medals on my bosom
at the War Mother's Convention.

No one knew my half-sister Dorothy was the real
Daughter of the American Revolution.

John followed me until he fell off that scaffold.
They carried him up the hill the day I turned up
the Ace of Spades next to the King of Hearts.

Esther Jane Craver (Helleny)

Some boys from over to Herrin came down
to look over the girls in Murphysboro.
The one they called Taffie had caramel skin
and melt-in-your-mouth eyes.
Ever since I was a young girl
I've had this here white streak
in my black hair, so I knew right off
he was going to be my husband.

That was a long time ago.
Now when I look in the mirror,
I say, "Hi Mom."
I told fortunes the same way she did
until my husband threatened to leave me.
We were walking down Walnut Street
when Maxine Louise from my sorority

asked me to read her palm.
"E. J.," he said, "I'm a business man.
I can't have that."

People believe anything you tell them
and they'll make it come true.
Then they say, "She's *good.*"
See these lines here?
I should have had many affairs.
Is my husband in bed?

Now I grow herbs and play
with my grandchildren.
But sometimes, when I wake at four,
I go out and read the stars.

To Aranyani

—Diane Cooledge Porter

I praise the musk-scented, fragrant, fertile, uncultivated
Aranyani, the mother of wild animals.—Rig Veda X, 146

Idle at wood's edge, I hear three notes,
high and thin as a filament of crystal,
from a towhee hidden in the safety of brambles.
Locust trees bristle with black fangs,
like a wild mother at bay,
defending what is left of her brood.

Scab trees, locusts cover wounded ground.
That's how the forest comes back.
But it will take longer than you or I
will live to see.

Shameless in the moist hollow of a leaf,
tree frogs tickle
the curvilinear wetlands of my inner ear.
Stepping carefully among fallen thorns, I penetrate
down to where a creek slips by
so slow and small that it makes no more sound
than a snake passing.

My hand touches the rude silk of horsetail grass,
socketed stems rising thick as green steam.

I know this grass,
fashioned when the forest
was a Paleozoic maid.
Now she is crone,
taken, cut so that men can raise corn
and do a thousand hard-edged things.

Flash of rusty red—the towhee has followed me.
It sails across an opening, twists tail midair,
and slips into a thicket of blackberries.

Neither am I a young woman any longer.
One crone to another,
I beg the forest, take me back.
Let me be your child again.

The Fox

—*Michelle Demers*

He leaps through
a familiar yellow field
mid-air, tail sailing
a face full of singing,
a body taut with complete attention.

Inside, I wait on my solitary cushion.
The sutra pulls me
with its eternal string
that leads to the bottom of a river.

Silence
without anticipation
hovers like a distant
circling hawk.

I want to fly
like the red fox
outstretched and reaching
for its catch.

My spine is vibrating,
a pathway for the running fox.

Sometimes

—*Tony Ellis*

sometimes
a light like molten fire
rushes through my veins
and a grin splits my face,
so certain
that I must know everything

sometimes
there is nothing so fulfilling
as the white tassel of a carpet
seen through the eyes of everything
or a simple green pot
sitting clean
on a perfect surface

Into the Woods

—Rolf Erickson

Heading north
just over
the ridge

you'll
find
the lake

wide as a world

deeper
than
mind
can
be

patiently
waiting
for

you alone

it's
your
home

it's where
your dreams go
to come true

it's the reason sometimes
not knowing why
you stop and listen

the trail
heads
north

into the woods

day
and
night

it calls you

Carrying Milk

—Rolf Erickson

Carrying new milk
across
fresh snow

as the warmth
of the barn
seeps

off into the night

I walk that
cold straight
golden line

cast out
by
our back porch light

where
inside
like always

someone waits

it's a
vast flat
wide white world

and in
my hands
I hold

like so many winters

as
an
offering

its essence

They Thought it Was a Dragon Kite
For Martha Ho

—*Diane Frank*

Waiting for the L
three blocks from the Pacific,
green wave crashing
down the slope to Taraval Beach,
they thought it was a dragon kite
but really it was a river
of old Chinese women.

Noisy flock of seagulls
arcs north toward the Headlands
above a spider web mesh
of electric wire.
Dragon kite flirts with pelican
above sand dollar
littered beach.

Flock of Cantonese women
in baseball caps
gathers at the bus stop,
chirps like paper cranes in a language
that floated here on wooden boats.

They fly on silver tracks
to Chinatown vegetable markets.

When I am ninety-eight years old,
I want to ride to Paradise
in a river of multi-ethnic women
singing in a kite of languages
on dragons with silver wings
lifting like Sun and Moon
to the apogee, then the edge
of a blue horizon.

Want to fly above silver tracks.
Don't want to ride there
on a streetcar!

Déjà Vu

—Diane Frank

Pumpkin soup
    with shitake mushrooms.

Chu-chu goes to sleep
    in her new dress.

Something about her presence
    allows me to feel
        my grief.

Eggplants roasting
    on the wood stove
        with sage, owl feather.

In my memory
    the contralto harmony of
        my mother's voice.

Light on the back
    of the head
        of a wooden bird.

Fourth of July in Fairfield, Iowa

—*Diane Frank*

Watching the fireworks with Nancy Berg,
I like the ones that fizzle
and fall into the reservoir.
The fireflies are confused, unfocused,
knocking their heads on the Queen Anne's lace.
The Pleiades have turned red
and now are slowly sinking beyond the horizon
like seven flamboyant women in the boys' shower.
Behind us the blonde haired farm girls are going wild.
Light another one! Light another one! Light another one!
Just like the Statue of Liberty holding a pinwheel.
Just like Niagara Falls spilling over Nancy's hair,
slinky fiddle music, turning to its own direction.
This one is dedicated to the computer nerds in Fairfield.
This one is the astronomy map in Pod 123,
mysterious candles on an exploding birthday cake,
a *Classics Illustrated* comic imploded into the future,
finally recognized, painted years ago
in defiance of *Mad Magazine* by Mrs. Berg.
Nancy's boyfriend buys us lemonade.
Afterwards, they will play on the swings,
go home, and not make love.

The frat boys from the edges of hell
toilet paper the elm tree by the courthouse.
I leave my windows open
and wait for flamingos
at four o'clock in the morning.

My Mother's Daughter

—*Diane Frank*

It is five years before I was born,
before life ruined her.

She is already sixteen years old,
breasts rising like yeasted bread,
which she tries to conceal on the streets
of her immigrant neighborhood,
but when she sings with Tommy Dorsey's Big Band,
she stuffs her dress with tissues,
paints her lips red,
and styles her hair like Judy Garland.

At Weequahic High School
she joins the hall patrol
to station herself outside the door
of my father's sixth period class.
She's smiling every afternoon
when he walks out of the door.

Later they escape to the West Village
in his red convertible

to the apartment he shares with his half brother
in a loft filled with etchings.

When he walks into the night club
where she pretends to be eighteen years old,
she sings to my father
directly with bedroom eyes,
How High the Moon
blasting out of Tommy's trombone
and then cascading from her mouth.
Who could resist such a song?

By the subway stop to Harlem
to see Billie Holiday,
he buys two gardenias for her hair.
A few months later,
they hitchhike to a cabin
by Caroga Lake in upstate New York,
share a bottle of wine,
throw the glasses into the fire
and create me.

On Location

—*Rodney Franz*

The train chants a *tarantella*
forsaking sun-soaked ruins
as we ride the bite of the devil.
There is lullaby locomotion
even in 6/8 time
and I grow sleepy
drunk with repetition
passing da Vinci hillsides—
soft-skinned seductions
lazing in frescoed succession
that become as common
as the film crew
chattering in my cabin.

An October as fresh as a tiny ball
of *mozzarella di bufalo*
exploding on first bite—
wet, delicate and white
inside my mouth.

Vagabond marshes
blur gray and khaki-green—

forgotten *"dammi una lira"* locales
sporadically spotted
by a phalanx of stiff armor and fumes
risen from demon seeds—
until on either side
tracks begin to multiply
and divide,
cutting the wetlands
with a heavy weave.

A slow drum roll
lurches into trochaic finale
inside the darkened terminus.
It's hard to tell
if the grime overhead covers windows
for the scene is as gray as an old newsreel.
With weekend bags in hand
aimed at weekday work
we jostle for space
over shadowy marble
combating the sports car verve
and spaghetti-fed vigor
of the anxious
all pressing to shed the vaulted gloom—
riveted, burnished and blistered—
dwarfing us,
forcing us to funnel

through narrow-gated escapes
following silhouetted pilgrims
backlit by dusty shafts of promise.

Once through—
the heart-ripping expanse
of baroque fanfare
crescendos into silence.
Tears cloud the beauty
of the Grand Canal.
Venice dressed in gold
as close to perfection as God's breath—
immediate and intimate courtesan
stunning me, wooing me
as she floats above her reflection
in the lapping, kissing waters.

Two Versions of the Self

—Glenn Freeman

I. MIND

The sky, set in its ways, refuses
to budge, thick overcast
hanging pregnant. Language
will not put your hands to the dark
underbellies like Braille, angles
of sunlight flooding through whatever
spaces will allow it, axles of light
shifting slowly, disappearing. Each moment
so thick with revision. The field of redwings
swells in its chorus of clicks & trills.
Will words then mirror, like the pond's
diffused reflection, hill & sky, dead
tamaracks in the cattails, or
are they the habitat of invention itself, soon enough
disappearing into something we can't
yet imagine, a heron into sticks, snow
into a field of snow, or these first drops of rain
striking the pond's calm surface?

II. BODY

Language will never put your hands
into the landscape, never offer the map
back to whatever place lives
in memory. Sometimes
we need to seize the words as if
they were wet clay, work them
with our fingers, shape, mold, form
some new understanding. Each moment
so thick with revision, language itself
becomes a character stepping
from the frame. I am no painter.
So I tell you the hill across the lake
is like a woman's hips as she curls on her side
by the fire, knees pulled slightly
toward her chest, and in that crook is the place
my hand most loves to rest, the dip
into the waist where a stream might run
when the rains begin to come.

The School

—*Glenn Freeman*

From shore, the swarm
    glides & flashes as one
        body the color

of disturbed water
    so the swell they ride
        looks already broken, frothy—

a single organism
    shifting & turning just
        beneath the surface in a way

that allows it to *become*
    the surface—sometimes
        erupting in silver spray,

other times submerged, visible
    only to pelicans
        & cormorants who dive

headlong into the ebbing tide
    where young boys stand
        in the shallows, tossing nets

seaward, dragging them
    and their bounty of perch
        & mackerel onto the sand,

an iridescent mass of individuals
    flipping & slapping as one
        being the way I imagine

the agitated mass of a brain
    in the midst of a convulsion,
        quivering solid turned fluid,

particle & wave, the way
    the mind says *Flame*
        even as it flits toward its own

dissolution: what can we know
    without losing ourselves
        like sailboats across the vast sea

of our own awareness,
    dragged on
        by who knows what wind.

November 1

—Glenn Freeman

All the dead
stubs of incense stick
from pots of rosemary,
violet & jade, tiny relics

as if the remains
of some fear long since
burnt to ash & smoke
still waft through the room

with the dust & cat hair the way
cigarette butts & half-empty, warm
beers concoct their own noxious smell
to eventually become

part of the house, some elemental
strand in the fabric like memories
becoming your life. Halloween
is wasted on the young. Now,

the spirits become more
palpable, like trinkets
you've kept all these years
just to be able to dust.

Meditation on a Mountainside

—*Glenn Freeman*

In Tibet, this would be the ultimate:
perched on cliffs where vultures gather.

We could be carrion, a feast, eaten, carried
higher, closer to god.

The faithful believe Christ
is a wafer and we're drunk on the teeth-

staining wine. I know a potter who throws pots
he believes contain the spirit: by shaping clay

he molds the very soul
the way vocabulary, syntax

shape the mind's possibilities. How
to explain a life without becoming

the explanation, tendrils of language
trailing away like a slug's slippery trail. *Happiness?*

Aristotle says all things move toward perfection,
a more durable joy, like the kernel of meaning

lodged inside the market's muddy dialect:
Joy, Cheer, All in the home products aisle

like perfect drugs to wash our spirits clean.
T used to tell me we could communicate

without words but what would we do
with all our time? Speech would become desire

for misunderstanding, a plot twist, anything
more interesting, the way

I toss stones at these ugly birds—our ticket,
supposedly, to that wordless paradise—just

to watch them lift, startled,
onto sweaty thermals with whatever

illusions we've laid on their wings.

Sanctuaries

—*Lois Grunwald*

It's the cat in the dry drainage
ditch I remember. Four girls at
the swimming hole,
the blue swing in the shade, a lone
cottonwood, dazzling as storefront diamonds,
a walk

home past a Heinz soup can, a plastic bag
ballooned in branches, serpentine
glance following us to

the drowned cat. That night
my father stirs Jack Daniels,
the heat leaving my back, my sun-burnt

cheeks through the glass bottom
shrink like a grey butterfly pinned
to a stem.

I go out the side door to friendly
stars. At the distant, still pond I imagine
the barn owl crossing the dark

cleft of sky to bend a branch while echoes
of a girl's laugh drop into
a hidden mouse's nest in the reeds. My uncle,

the other alcoholic, is kind
as my father's eyes are lost. His Pall
Mall jacket rubs my hair. I hear
him say, *Lolly*.

Signposts, 1

—*Lois Grunwald*

Something made us hop across Wallace Creek to find the young
man camped for six days in the same spot, nursing blisters and running

a hand through his red hair, cerulean eyes ablaze as he told
us of days spent hiking in every direction there at the headwaters

of the Kern. Morning sun lit up his yellow tent like a beacon, and we
rubbed our hands, skittering in place to keep warm in air growing
  colder by
the day. He talked so nonchalantly of scaling peaks and passes that
  I imagined

he was John Muir's ghost greeting hikers who slog past this obscure
crossroads on their way to a wind-blown lake. We had seen no

one, after all, for two days, save the fisherman coaxing a horse with
  rolling
eyes down the stony, steep path. The man was headed

up the Kern to camp somewhere in a day's worth of Jeffrey pine
and red fir. Wallace Creek was only a foot deep but in the spring it's
  a torrent

that halts hikers along the John Muir Trail for a month or more. It
   cascaded past
empty, forlorn campsites, the damp air sinking into us as Mars

and Saturn, like solitary sentinels, flanked the waning moon. It was
   September.
There was no one there. They'd left to sit between stuccoed walls to
   stare at a phone
they hope won't ring or maneuver

for a parking space at Wal-Mart where they are transfixed for a
moment before
the cool, white space of the building's outer wall that has turned gold

in the sun's last light. It gives them a sense of peace they can't explain,
and then they remember the dipper at the stream's edge, how it slid
   in a tiny

rapid, bobbed out, and vanished in the glassy depths, or the frogs in
   the tarn
at 12,000 feet that slipped away from an intruder like leaves scattering

in the wind, or the ones that didn't move at all, but merged
with the muddy bottom, as if
it was home.

Signposts, 2

—*Lois Grunwald*

In the middle of the journey of our life I came to myself within a dark wood
where the straight way was lost
                    —Dante Alighieri, The Divine Comedy

The sky is strange—clouds fly along distant ridges,
and for now, here among the Sierra's highest peaks,
it is clear and bitterly cold. We climb the ridge

because we must. It is the way to another basin, another
camp, then home. There is no path, just massive

talus, steep sand. Fear is not my worst enemy. It sleeps
with me. I stroke its burned flanks until it no longer peers
with blood red eyes.

I was lost once in the woods. What I remember is the panic
of enveloping green, the pellucid creek, the human voice
finally heard.

Malefic violet-grey clouds descend into wedges
of sunlight left on boulders, blades of grass. Thunder
follows. We make it to a hollow

in the lodgepole pines. The first flakes fall, soon become
a whiteout. The season's first snowfall. It will likely melt,
but I cannot see that, cannot see the translucent
day. There is just opaque

ground, the smothered sky. You say, *we need
water*, and bolt down through the meadow. The stream is too
far. I follow and look back to see our small blue
tent fade into white.

Repairs

—*Dianna Henning*

The sock fit over a darning egg,
compliant with whatever hand lavished attention.
How loved the sock must have felt
held by the darner. If
the hole was more than three stitches
sewing thread instead of yarn
wove the delicate framework
to heal the sock, the frayed strands
gathered in, tucked back. This required
a tapestry needle with a large eye
big enough to see, to thread.
Don't ask if the foot recognized
such care, or if someone forgot
not only the socks you darned,
but also the slippers you brought to his sickbed.
You must be a weaver of sorts to darn.
Someone who bridges empty space with possibility.

The Butcher's Apprentice

—*Dianna Henning*

First he showed him how to hold the cleaver,
where to make the best cut,
said to keep his eye on the meat's grain,
hold the blade steady,
and how beautifully the meat opened
on the maple chopping block,
gracious host to its own body,
the apprentice wiping his bloodied hands
across his heavy cotton apron;
his sigh, such finesse,
a sigh a lover might make,
satisfied before ultimate
pleasure—but, no climax here,
only the calm of knowing
one did the other body right,
and can't you tell
that the one being trained
seeks the best advice to finish meat,
especially since fine butchery is nearly extinct,
for why else
would the Master train
the hand coming back to fingers,

to opening, carefully at first,
the red inner flesh that was once desire.

What You Have

—Dianna Henning

Dying is a white room where you feel most holy.
There are no curtains,
no ornaments, no bric-a-brac to distract,
no rugs on the floor.
Here, the texture of air
is a cool leaf.

Like Frida, who painted herself as a deer,
you were a feeling before you became a thought.
You scrape your head on silence,
pull arrows from your temples.

Remember how the nuns floated into line,
their long apprenticeship
to the eternal—how small tremors of breath
pulsed down their backs?

You want to become holy like the nuns,
to feed on the word.
You shoo a fly from your nose,
surprised it darts about

in the high voltage
of the sacred.

Dying isn't easy,
but it's all you've got.

Eight Years Old in Sarajevo
(prompted by an NPR broadcast)

—*Tom Kepler*

The shell explodes, snaps back
her teacher's head, chalks the board
with brains and blood, clots of hair.

A table, a tablet, pencil, eraser.
Her best friend, an apple wrinkling,
disappears within the sound.

Tree limbs thin and fork.
Elbows and pockets, thumbs and eyes.
Christmas spruce, children's shoes.

She dreams of running, running
through craters of shadow and light,
walks asleep on legs she's lost, walks

to the front of the class to recite.
She is writing a poem with her class
when the window of the image explodes,

first lines fragmenting into last.
Dream or scream, the red rubble
of her legs trail like runes across her rhyme.

Words for My Son

—*Tom Kepler*

Words, like wood, will warm the evening air.
We settle, coals within our bed,
blanketed thigh by thigh,
light ruddy with our words.

Your hand rises like woodsmoke into my hair.
Words twine and twist, shadows gather,
and in the shadows, spiders weave their patient webs.

Listen to the words as they crackle and pop,
whole pages flaring, flames thumbing
rough-barked logs, stars craning overhead,

reading over our shoulders words illuminated,
banked with marrow of meaning enough
to warm us through the long, cold night.

Even when the words die back,
the stones of our bodies retain a lingering heat.
We read, bones bright with meaning,
cool to a wordless sleep.

Tsunami Notebook

—poems washed up from the sea of tears—2005
—Robin Lim

Have you wondered why all the windows in heaven were broken?
Have you seen the homeless in the open grave of God's Hand?
—Kenneth Patchen

Notes Taken Flying Low and Slow on a Red Cross Plane

First the earthquake
and the women trying to save their kitchen glass.
The men regretted their broken aquariums
tenderly they lifted the fish into plastic bowls for safety.

There were some minutes of peace.
The mothers serving morning rice.
Sunday market bustling.
The sea receded and the prices dropped
as old men walked out, to pick fish
like fallen fruit around the feet of trees in season.

While chewing and haggling the people heard
the ocean explode.
Explode like a bomb.

Then he, Neptune, or some bastard adolescent son of the sea god
began to roar.

He came as a hot black wall
with stinking breath
and white cobra teeth.

Tsunami, we later called him,
came from many directions,
pushing trees, buildings, cars, mothers, cousins,
babies, wooden cabinets—full of everything we had,
five kilometers inland.

The scrap metal that cut
Rizky's cheek
decapitated his father.
Rizky, eight orbits old,
let go of his father and found a wooden plank
which carried him upcountry in the flood.
His cousin floated on an upholstered couch in comfort
but it was sucked back out to sea. Gone.

Sarjani's six-year-old daughter was torn
from her arms.
All the mothers repeat and repeat the story

of not holding onto the baby.
A caribou offered her horn
and swam to the surface. An old cow
dragging a pregnant woman skyward,
to leave her by the roof of the Masjid.
She gave birth that evening, right on the roof of that Mosque.
Seventy people found refuge there,
imagine that one would be a birthing woman,
another a midwife.
When the water receded, they lowered the baby down
in a black plastic bag.

In the rubber forest you will find "Search and Rescue"
workers, and survivors. Every day they look for people,
after two months they still find fifteen bodies, twenty bodies.
They don't worry about where to dig, wherever they dig,
bones and a little flesh, torn garments to be recognized,
wait to be found. Why do people wait for prayers?
The animals, those not in cages,
quietly walked upcountry, when the earthquake began.
Somehow they expected the sea to be drunk with anger,
and so they left.

To Love a Wife

—*Robin Lim*

Bang Hanafi had a wife. She visited his leaf-enhanced dreams
to tell him where to find their baby daughter.
She told him, to dig under a tree,
by a shaft of sunlight, where she and the baby were waiting.
He led his few friends with picks, an old shovel, to the deep mud.
When she was uncovered, he said she was beautiful.
In her life she was black and thin. She had wished to be
plump, and white, and now she has grown big, pale.
I only wish I had some fragrant oil,
to help her smell a little better.

Roti Aceh

—Robin Lim

They call this bread... roti
spun from precious sugar,
boiled in coconut milk,
pounded from rice,
woven with hands which swam the tsunami waters,
and somehow lived.
And somehow, painted red with henna, remembered how to cook.

The veiled women send this 'bread of Aceh'
like skeins of golden cord, tightening
around my life.
It pulls me back to the clinic,
to unhealed wounds,
unattended sorrows,
merciless dreams of remembering baby daughters.

This sweetened thread loaf
ties me to sleep on hard packed Sumatran sand
where 500,000 recently dead souls
are also trying to sleep.

The women, picking seaweed from their black hair,
packed this witch-bread in a box of prayers,
heaven's banquet labeled, "operation blessing."

He is not my most beautiful child,
this last one from my body—
copper, copper, red, pink, rusty penny boy.
He is the child of the truest and unexpected
love of my life.
The love that rings in the bells of my body
and wakes me like an earthquake.
Spills like water
from one flooded rice field to all the fields
freshly planted below.
A spreading deep green glass floor
reflecting storms.

In Aceh I saw the end of the world,
the rainbow promise of a senile God, broken.
We can never fix it, or mend even one sorrow
by sharing grief or forgiving ourselves for still living.
Enough,
the bird still sings and I pray for my own children.

What Will Never Dry

—*Robin Lim*

On the beach at Meulabouh
54 days after the tsunami
I found a seaman's hat
just coming ashore, home without the sailor.
Two twisted tricycles,
plastic torn from soup packages,
a little bit of hand-crocheted shawl.
A boy's shoe, size seven, with no sole.
A hermit crab living in a perfect shell.
A rusty broken military tower, looking West.
The sun is setting upon a peaceful glass-table-top green and silver sea.

Behind me is a mass grave and a Mosque still standing.
God, what does that mean? In nearly every village,
and broken seaside city, the arched Mosques
with onion-shaped copper crowns still gleam in the day,
stand proud and mostly white.
The Indian Ocean tenderly sprays my face with his salty spit.
I am aroused by his breath in my ears, and so I walk forward a step
until I am wet.
He is warm, the temperature of tears.

Artifacts of Death

—Robin Lim

My beautiful son, baked black,
home from the tsunami waters
where he and his brother and some old farts
towed donated fishing boats
to villages who lost all.
They had 300 boats,
but they need only one or two now
because they lost most of their people.
The dead don't eat fish.
Quite the opposite

Thor shows me a collection, gifts from Acehnese survivors—
an old war bayonet, used to kill many rebels.
His sweaty hand opens to show me tiger's teeth.
He unfolds a plastic body bag, sees my eyes
and says, "Don't worry mom, it's never been used."

I send my sons to Aceh; this is their school,
"Earthquake High,"
where the sea eats everything loved.

The Buddha sat under a tree, attacked by his own fear of death,
or fear of life,
until every sword that pierced his heart
became a flower.
He had it easy.
I immerse my children in annihilation.
They come home to show me what remains.
Is the heart indestructible,
or do we burnish it shiny, to the density of stone?
What kind of mother have I become?
I give them bitter learning and cruel medicine.
They come home and hug me.

Eden

—Sharon Long

At the zoo,
between the elephants
and the aviary,
we walked the asphalt path,
I, deep in a purple suit polka-dotted white,
you with August melting at your throat.

We paused by the honeysuckle dripping with bees,
pressed palm to damp palm,
and the caw caw of the cockatoo
plummeted through green, ripe,
summer-lush leaves,
and sunk into my womb.

Then longing stretched out to
every cage and every prowling beast,
to every creature of veldt or tundra,
to every crawler and growler and restless pacer,
to the sky and to the sun and to the earth,

and to you throwing popcorn at the polar bears,
you leaving spun, pink, sticky

cotton-candy threads
on the skin of my wrist and jaw,

and to beige dust
silent under the elephant's lifted foot.

Brushfire

—*Joy Lyle*

There were tracks in the garden.

The rain a hand
dispersed, the soil
was never dirty.
My mother held the screen door open
to view the soundless animals
refuged in rows of carrots.
From his kitchen chair, my father aimed
and shot: a drum beat,
the spring cried, the door slapped shut.
Come autumn, come rain, the grass
shimmered, the field shook off
its green dress.
The rain extinguished the fire.
From inside the hollow stubble the fire

reappears—

a child at the door—
gingers out an old log:
a crocodile, a kayak, family pictures
left unpacked, the fire

overturns
acre by acre going.

The redhead sways her hair over her shoulder.

We see best what we see from afar.
                                        Close your eyes.
The damper on the stove turned down.
A young girl sees a woman singed.
                                        A yellow bus halts—
passengers dismount.
What doesn't move
hurts and holds.

The Washer Woman Moves
Away from Herself

—*Joy Lyle*

She washed and ironed twelve white tablecloths,
borrowed china from the church, cut flowers
from a nearby roadside for the tables.
Having someone see her could have saved her.
She filled the salt and pepper shakers.
Put to roast five legs of lamb with celery.
Carried the clean laundry from the cellar,
folded and tucked it into the drawers.
Buffed the floors and fixed the garbage disposal.
Polished her shoes and the tabletops.
Determined Sunday the handiest day as no one
would leave work early nor children miss a day of school.
Sewed the missing buttons on her dresses.
Got her garments through the washer and ringer
and hanging straight on time. She ordered harp music.
Set the chairs in the direction she wanted people to face.
She wrote it down: a date of birth, a family name.
These could be hers or someone else's
and no one would know.
She'd been told: stay inside. Stay. Stay.
We weren't looking and she left, wanting

to take herself with her
but she was more than she could pack.
And couldn't find her way back in
once the backdoor screen had pulled itself shut.

Idleness Leads to Astronomy

—*Matthew MacLeod*

Galileo shuts his eyes.
All night he ponders the universe,
all day he sleeps lightly in dream theories.
Now it is day as he lies on the grass of a Parisian Park,
early morning, covered in dew and regrets
of never learning to dance.
He transcends the calls of birds,
the smell of walnut trees, the intricacies
of light that brighten the inner eyelid
and the casual song of a cobblestone musician's cello
being tuned.

Mid-day he sleeps heaviest in bright sunlight,
wishes his mind would rest like the planets.
Ants that have drunk half a mug of abandoned black coffee
crawl over him from blades of grass—
across his bare feet, up his trousers, over
his sweated forehead, eyebrow, earlobes, even lips!
He dreams the Lilliputians are tying him down:

They have come, he theorizes, into Paris,
along the Seine, from the Martinique.

They have come, he theorizes,
in sailboats made from toothpick-masts,
fringe sails and walnut shells!

A Storyteller

—*Courtney McDermott*

I am the only visitor to Ada Petrie's room
    Not so much her visitor as her audience
She's old and crippled
In the county nursing home
Everyday she sits by her windowsill
Overlooking the cement courtyard
Wearing a peach dressing gown and
Worn-in sweatdrabbed red silk slippers
With gold and violet stitchings of flowers and bonsai trees
She tells me the story of those slippers every visit
How they were bought
From an outdoor shop in NYC Chinatown
For a paper-Lincoln from a squat woman in lavender linen.
    And about how everything nowadays is imported
    And a five-dollar bill won't buy you shit.
She talks of her goatfarm
About making cheese and butter with nothing more
Than a battered pine churn from the Civil War era
And her own pair of liverspotted gnarled hands
Where you could make your own food
    And not buy processed packaged plastic
    Food from a supermarket

She reminisces for a country barndance
With fiddles and moonshine and big red taffeta skirts
And a man named Jerry Jeffers who looked like a god
    And she hums and taps her foot
    And she gets real quiet
And then I am forgotten like the unremembered dead.

Driving Good Gifts into Hiding

—Connie Larson Miller

There is a place along the river
where he commands cottonwoods
silent. But he couldn't keep them
from whispering.

Just as he plowed our prairie,
we woke to the want
of milkweed and falcon.

I pull cornhusks
from my sleeves
along the Interstate
spreading from town
into greedy blacktop.
And he snatches a dime
from the pig lot.

There was a woman
who offered up her suffering
so that her children
would have faith.
The poor have such a luxury.

How to Kill Longing

—*James Moore*

First, collect all your corpuscles and place them in a mixing bowl,
stirring gently till you reach the desired consistency.

Second, arrange bite-sized mounds evenly across a lightly greased
  baking tin.
  (Butterscotch chips may be added.)

Third, preheat the oven to 350 degrees. Place tray on top rack.
Bake for approximately 12-15 minutes.

Fourth, remove from oven and let sit for 10 minutes.

When the cookies have sufficiently cooled,
place them neatly in the wastebasket.

Or, simply put your head in the oven and turn on the gas.
(Do not try this at home.)

Passamezzo

—Susie Niedermeyer

Black as China tea it hovers
in a corner, one ebony wing
outstretched. Sometimes a few strings
sound like the faintest moan
of a woman dreaming, and when the cat
walks placidly down its perfect spine
discordant notes protest.
But when she sits to play, the *adagio*
of the yellow day pours in
and a few notes rise from the sleepy tangle
of clefs and bar lines to float on the river
of light. Hands reach and leap
in undulant feline play, lithe as dancers
as she rocks into the arch of phrases.
Strands of hair fall into her face
and the final passage spills like rain
that rises in tendrils from the earth
wrapping the fields around her. Weary now
she sees only the collapsed pale spiders
of her hands, mute carriers of song,
a glaze of perspiration on the keys.

Anniversary

—Kassy Scrivner

"I have a toy pony. It takes big shits," a boy said.
He climbed up a rock and peed into Main Street.
The fat lady walking by stopped and began to sing.
Grandpa Albert lost his teeth again.
Aunt Cindy stole Bob's credit cards and bought a naked rat.
The cat was cataleptic.
Marilyn lost her birth certificate and was deported.
John finally shaved his legs and put on a dress.
A kangaroo court sentenced Uncle Howie for hunting nude.
Carol built a nuclear reactor and buried it in the backyard.
The dog licked Jacinda's toes while she drank green tea.
Mary Poppins smoked like a chimney.
The bull and the horse perverted the piazza.
Fat people in Minnesota ate the cows.
Five-legged frogs with three eyes procreated in the river.
When I was six I got lost in a funeral home.
The dog watched Apryl undress, I think she liked it.
Dead people are mannequins.
The panda was in heat, so was the emu.
Geraldine had no teeth and ate a duck's bill at Lake Fair.
Lepers saw dead people.
We danced naked on Thursdays and skinny-dipped on Wednesdays.

A paisley jacket stood up a pair of purple stockings.
The can opener broke opening tuna when the doorbell rang.
You sent me flowers.

Prediction

—Christine Seddon

They say the snow is coming. My knees stiffen
as a black cat weaves through the porch rail;
slacken when my neighbor drops his blinds
to let me know he's home. I drink limes to feel the sun.
Pass time watching rain thicken to a streak of glass

as the bee slows to a clumsy death. I know what follows.
How I'll speak in softer tones; stand still as night
deafened by the sound of crickets
and thrashing leaves. How the cosmos will freeze
like angels stunned by their fall from grace.

Stone Cold

—Christine Seddon

Even the trees stand still,
a thousand deer waiting
ears pricked for twigs snapping
underfoot, and the human scent
that follows. Down here

everything is harder. Woolen socks on the line
stiffen with ice as the earth closes in
like a stricken child. Only a few pumpkins
pocked by hail and vermin teeth
continue to soften inside.

My Sister's Needle

in memory of Kathy Lynch Mueller—1939-1996

—*Margaret Siskow*

On the eve of Independence,
in a dark corner
of your crowded storage room,
I find the scarf
you had hoped to finish.

Your silver needle rests
half in, half out
in the middle of a running stitch
across red and blue sparklers.

I fold it like altar cloth,
careful that the needle remain
exactly as you left me.

Your silenced sentence
left behind in a box
marked "Goodwill."

The Chinese Tapestry

—*Gladys Swan*

It hangs on our wall now, this tapestry,
a century old or more, worn once
for a wedding—that great occasion—
folded in a trunk perhaps, the treasure
of some family before a change of fortune
or meaning shook it loose
into a peddler's hands.

From a band of red and black horizons
vines twine and leaf their gold;
down spear points alternating red and green
that fringe the scene below gold emblems
draw the eye to birds, flowers, leaves—
embroidering the world again
on black ground.

At the center, a tall-masted ship
draws a small boat, with a man and woman
on the way to destiny: from virginity
to marriage, even as it sails from dream
to waking, life to death; dolphins leap
on either side.

Shall I say how difficult it was
to give it space? The images on our walls
we took down one by one and shifted all about.
But even with the first blank space
the house tilted on its axis,
let in a whiff of chaos: vertigo.

It all starts with the pleasure of seeing,
the seduction. I stand like a stunned ox,
called by its radiance
into the mind-moving image captured
in a frame: to step into chance and change,
all that passes through its golden gleam.

It too has sailed beyond its moorings—
even as the ship came west
across the seas—beyond its moment,
its occasion, to rest here on the wall,
speaking its illumination.

Schoodic Cove: Unorganized Territory

—Gladys Swan

What do I think of first? The lake, with its
shadows and reflections, its wild shore—
the loon calls that bear it to the moon
those nights at the full when all is cry
and echo? The two sentinel white pines
back of the path by the old privy?
The hermit thrush that tunes the silence
of the woods to its own measure?

The swamp, for instance, where the snags
are stripped down to arrows, pointing
at all angles. Like rotten teeth their roots
lose hold, and they fall to float their death
that is no death: grass shoots up;
laurel finds a home; pitcher plants,
blue asters in late summer—each log
nurse to a burgeoning world.

One year lightning struck the white pine
on the point, shattering half
the bifurcated trunk. Fragments
floating everywhere. Yet still it lives.

All this rises to the surface, my mind
a keep where I am kept, inadvertent
lover that I am. The kiss planted
by the eye comes back to claim me—
till I can bear no separation.
It has taught me longing.

What the Day Brings

—Gladys Swan

Unless it's pouring rain, the road I take
lies toward Katahdin, even if it's veiled
by cloud—toward its imprint,
deep blue against the sky—
as though it were a destination
I had to reach to validate the day.

Outposts on the way: the brook
winding through the woods
along a stony track—the rocks
glanced by sun; the water, shifting
transparencies of light. To pause there
is to enter its dark quiet, the trickle
of water, the slowness of time,
to let go the sediment
of wasted moments.

Then on to the railroad track
curving round the bend. Waiting
sometimes for the cars to clatter by,
whistle shrilling—the engineer waving.
Crossing where generations of kids

have laid their pennies on the track,
Abe Lincoln's cheek
against the cold steel.

What the day brings: moose tracks
on the road; bear or coyote scat;
a tree fallen across, sent by the wind.
A sudden find of blueberries alongside
or raspberries, spendthrift daisies,
black-eyed susans; fireweed in flame.
Among the tree roots
a treasure of chanterelles.

All of it shaping space and time
toward the possible eye.
Landscape, home of beginnings,
evocations—from the things themselves,
shape and color before the name.
A gathering to take to the mountain,
the sensual bouquet of being there:
eyes rising to its eminent form.

Lyrebird Song

—*Janet Thomas*

I was born near a forest of rags
where gum leaves droop in blistering sun,
and crackling dryness
starves whistling kites, flying foxes,
and frill-necked lizards.

Learning to love like a lyrebird,
I mimicked wattlebirds, lorikeets,
and empty-headed cockatoos.
Tea-time laughter came in white china cups,
familiar antidote to life's sudden venom.

The day my mother died,
my tongue floated in blood.
Blind words became rumbling rocks,
thrown at darkened windows.

A barrage of bellbirds splintered
the silver spittle of siblings
at her grave.
And when we planted a single boronia
in the orange ground,
a lyrebird sang the rain.

Trees Sing My Mother

—Janet Thomas

Radiant rainforest air raced
around you, my massive mother.
We firebrats scorched your bark,
and blood-wood orchids sprouted
white, violet, and magenta.

But when outlaw stranglers grew
snakes of suffocating stems,
you began to rot
inside your fig-root prison.

Frozen eyes followed a green python
slinking over your spongy spine,
while the blunt beaked wind
echoed our wordless prayer.

For forty days before the end
fire termites feasted, forming
your jackhammer mound of pain.

Then, my mother,
we found the ghost gum

by the ancient billabong,
and it blossomed
with a hundred white corellas.

Morning: Three Trees

—*Janet Thomas*

I

Grandma told me Daddy
stammers because
he was hiding in the orange tree
when the circus elephant leaned
over the back fence
and swallowed his voice.

II

I flew up the gum tree
when Mum's broomstick
caught my knuckle.
I saw smashed skin,
bone underneath.
On the ground,
Joe killed a black chook,
plucking its bloody feathers,
one by one.

III

Yellow maple
magpie—mad in March wind.
Fearless four year old
climbing too high.
Blue canvas sneaker
in that tiny fork.
I breathe.

Syphilis and Chocolate

—Viktor Tichy

I. Jewish Piano Builder

Grandpa Rudolf shot holes in the sky
instead of the gray wool on Russian chests.
He knew how to aim to avoid anybody,
and when to jump out of the trench,
hands above his head.

In the military hospital, he put his coins
on many eyes,
and fixed anything except the heart
of one woman without faith.
The Russian cure for syphilis was a bullet,
but only he could run the boiler in the basement
without blowing up the building.

Seven years after the war ended,
my mother was born. Grandma wanted to jump
under a train with her child,
but the Jewish doctor was kind
and both blood tests were negative.

Rudolf slept in the cellar
and ate out of a special dish.
He didn't build any more pianos
because every board warped in the damp air.
He taught his daughter how to read and write
but didn't dare to touch her.
In his last years she had to show him
how to spell his own name.

Grandma worked in a factory
to feed the family. More than music,
the world needed to make machines
for a better war.
But Rudolf's illness was faster.
He died naturally.

II. Christian Watchmaker

Every winter our house in Prague
smelled of baking cookies
and apples drying in the cellar. Then, one day
when darkness chased us from the ski slopes,
I found sparklers and candles on a pine tree,
a bucket of water beside the presents,
and Uncle Joe in my bed.

He didn't have a drop of Jewish blood.
He was Grandma's nephew, so I got the floor.
Joe always brought a huge box of candy
and hung the tin-wrapped chocolates
on the lower branches of our Christmas tree.
He would be tall as our father, he said,
but when he was a boy, all the milk and fish
were sent to the German soldiers
who were fighting the Russians and the Jews.

Instead he got a plaster bed
Cast by a Christian doctor,
but it was so hard, Joe never slept in it.
His spine grew twisted like a stalk of Morning Glory.
His face covered with fleshy growths
and he joked he could shave as close as a turkey,
but it wasn't catching.
His watchmaker eyes were full of mischief,
brown, and warm as the Christmas chocolates
melting in our mouths—
and we knew how catching love was.

All his clothes had to be custom made;
no uniform could fit his grotesque frame.
Joe was too ugly to die
for any ideology.
He once had a girlfriend who couldn't see well.

They prepared a wedding, but she left the day before
with all the clocks and watches of his clients.

He never called the cops.
He got a job in the power plant instead,
dried his eyes by the coal fire,
and paid for all the lost watches.
He wore his new tuxedo for the first time
to his funeral.

Now I have no Christian uncles left,
and the Jewish ones were consumed by a different fire.
I never cried for any of them
except the one so special
he was cremated in the coffin for a child.

I Thought About Her

—*Tova Vitiello*

For a long time, I thought about her,
alone, listening to Mahler.
She is thirty-one and growing tired.
Perhaps that is why she loses things:
books, lovers, a red scarf.

For a long time, I thought about
the artist who wears blankets from Peru,
her head bound in a kerchief
to keep it from slipping away.

For a long time, I thought about her.
When she wakes in the night
and walks barefoot across the floor,
who will call her back
or reach out a hand?

Walking with the Moon

—Tova Vitiello

It is late when she offers to walk with me
beneath snowflakes and street lights.
Stepping without pause through the cold,
we move in synchrony, elbow to elbow.
As we walk, I watch snow drift and settle
on rooftops, on pavement, on her tangled hair.

I wonder what attracts me to this woman
who lives in a world of mountains
and meditation, canoes and tea?

It is midnight when we arrive at my door.
Standing in silence, I feel
her fingers smooth the rough edges
of my wind-scratched face, and then
she disappears into the night.
Somewhere, she is walking with the moon.

In the Bowery

—*Tova Vitiello*

Men with unshaven faces
and nicotine tongues
sing songs of blessed Mary
as they stumble into traffic
to wash car windows
for our spare change.

A dime, a quarter…a cigarette….

As the hours stagger
from morning to night
one by one
they crouch
into some lampless corner
with a whiskey bottle
clutched to their chests
like a glass crucifix.

Awakening

—Tova Vitiello

Daylight trembles in the room
where she squeezes
and shoves twenty-six years
into paper bags
and cardboard boxes.

She is tired
of cautiously arranging
his shirts, his socks,
her words.

She is tired
of long hours in the kitchen
the smell of gas
ready to explode.

This morning, she awakes
and reaches for the kettle
the one with scratches and dents
the one that doesn't whistle
as it sits on the burner.

For the first time,
she sees the walls crack open
and hears
the water boil over
while the heat of her womb
is snuffed out.

Colonoscopy

—*Patricia Wellingham-Jones*

Camera mile deep
inside my body, I lie
on my left side,
eyes on the screen.
Boosted by Versed
and Demerol I slide
along slick pink walls.
With the camera I swing
around a deep bend,
swirl in tiny swoops of the lens,
ride joyously among luscious
rosy cavern walls.
I want to reach out,
trail my fingers along
the glistening convolutions,
hear myself giggle
at a dizzying dip.
Later, when the surgeon's
smiling voice proclaims
everything's normal
I think in my drifting way
this colon hasn't been so clean
since I was a four-month fetus.

Author Bios

Jillian Barnet's poetry has appeared in *North American Review, Nimrod, Bellingham Review,* and elsewhere, and her work has been nominated for a Pushcart Prize. Jillian received her M. F. A. from Vermont College in 2003. She is Coordinator of the David Berg Center for Ethics and Leadership at the University of Pittsburgh.

Elinor Benedict has published several chapbooks and a collection of poetry, *All That Divides Us,* which won the May Swenson Poetry Award from the Utah State University Press in 2000. She was founding editor of *Passages North* literary magazine.

W. E. Butts received the 2006 Iowa Source Poetry Book Prize for his collection, *Sunday Evening at the Stardust Café,* and is also the author of a chapbook, *Sunday Factory,* from Finishing Line Press. He is co-editor of the literary journal *Crying Sky.*

Michael Carrino is a graduate of the M. F. A. Program in Writing at Norwich University/Vermont College, Montpelier, VT. One of the co-founders and the Poetry Editor for the *Saranac Review,* he has three published books of poetry and has had work featured in *Scrivener, Hudson Review, Hayden's Ferry Review, Poet & Critic,* and other publications. He lectures in the English Department, State University College at Plattsburgh, NY.

Suzanne Cody lives in Iowa City with her daughter, Isabel.

Michelle Demers lives and writes in Williston, Vermont. She holds an M. F. A. from Vermont College and has been published in *Collecting Moon Coins II, Diner, The Dryland Fish, The Blue Fig Review,* and *Busenhalter* among other publications. She teaches poetry and writing at Saint Michael's College, the Community College of Vermont, New England Culinary Institute, the University of Vermont, and local community centers.

Tony Ellis is an Iowa-based writer and poet. His first book of poetry, *There is Wisdom in Walnuts,* won a Chelson scholarship prize in 2004. His second book, *The Morning Tree,* is due for publication in 2007. Samples of his work can be seen at his website: www.tonyellis.com.

Rolf Erickson writes poetry inspired by nature and consciousness. Significant influences include Robert Frost, Gary Snyder, and William Stafford. He also writes comedy, press releases, and love notes to his wife, Renee.

Diane Frank is author of five books of poems. Her friends describe her as a harem of seven women in one very small body. She lives by the Palace of Fine Arts in San Francisco—where she dances, plays cello, teaches writing workshops, and creates her life as an art form. Her first novel, *Blackberries in the Dream House,* was nominated for the Pulitzer Prize.

Rodney Franz is the Artistic Director of the Iowa Theatre Company. He has acted in film and television in London and Rome and is the author of three plays and a screenplay.

Glenn Freeman received an M. F. A. from Vermont College and a PhD in American Literature from the University of Florida. He teaches at Cornell College and lives in Cedar Rapids, Iowa with his wife and two cats.

Lois Grunwald lives with her husband, Spencer, in the foothills of Los Padres National Forest along the southern California coast. She is working on her M. F. A. in Writing (Poetry) from Vermont College.

Dianna Henning has published in: *Swink Magazine*, (online); *Asheville Poetry Review; Seattle Review; The Spoon River Poetry Review; Red Rock Review; Psychological Perspectives; The Louisville Review; Crazyhorse & South Dakota Review*. Her book *The Tenderness House* was published by Poets Corner Press '05, Stockton CA. Check out her website: www.thompsonpeakretreat.com. She was a three-year recipient of a *California Arts Council* residency grant.

Tom Kepler is a faculty member of Maharishi School of the Age of Enlightenment in Fairfield, Iowa. He has previously published in a half dozen or so literary magazines, including *The Hiram Poetry Review, Wind, California Quarterly, Riverrun*, and *The Galley Sail Review*.

Joy Lyle has an M. F. A. degree from the University of Iowa's Writers' Workshop. Her poems have been published in *Poetry Northwest, The Sewanee Theological Review, Mid-American Review, Cutbank, Poet Magazine*, and other publications. She lives on a farm near Keota, IA with her husband Trent and teaches poetry writing at Indian Hills Community College in Ottumwa, IA.

Matthew MacLeod is a poet and songwriter from Canada currently living in Australia. His poems have been previously published in *Scrivener, Scribe,* and *Lyrical Iowa.* His anthology of poems by contemporary Iowa poets, *The Dryland Fish,* won the Chelson prize for best work of poetry 2003.

Courtney McDermott is a native of New Hampton, Iowa. She graduated from Mount Holyoke College in 2005 and has (briefly) lived in Ireland, Los Angeles and Minneapolis. Currently, she is working on a novel and applying to the Peace Corps.

Connie Larson Miller lives in southeastern Iowa and teaches throughout the state for VSA Arts Iowa. She has previously been published in *Lyrical Iowa, Dryland Fish, Eclipsed Moon Coins,* and *Iowa Heritage.*

James Moore is a freelance writer, lifelong musician, co-host of the Fairfield Film for Thought Series, and station manager of KRUU-LP, a non-profit grassroots community radio station. He has been featured as a guest editorialist in a number of regional newspapers and is co-author of a self-help ebook. His poetry has appeared in *Modern Drummer, Punk Debris, Lyrical Iowa* and his girlfriend's hand.

Susie Niedermeyer is by education a classical pianist, but her poetry has been published in journals and magazines including *The MacGuffin, Lyrical Iowa,* and *The Sierran Magazine.* In addition she won 2nd place in a contest sponsored by the National Federation of

State Poetry Societies in 2002 and had two poems featured in *The Dryland Fish*, an anthology of contemporary Iowa Poets, published in April 2004.

Kassy Scrivner is a recent graduate of the University of Redlands where she received her Bachelor of Arts in Studio Art, Poetry, and Small Business Administration. She is currently in the process of obtaining her M. F. A. in writing at Vermont College. Originally from Oregon, Ms. Scrivner now lives outside of Los Angeles.

Christine Seddon received her M. F. A. in Writing from Vermont College. She has published work in *Vermont Magazine* and currently lives in Burlington, Vermont.

Gladys Swan is both a writer and a visual artist. She has published two novels, *Carnival for the Gods* and *Ghost Dance: A Play of Voices*, as well as six collections of short fiction, the most recent being *A Garden Amid Fires*. She has been nominated twice for the PEN/Faulkner Award and has received the Tate Prize for Poetry from the *Sewanee Review*.

Viktor Tichy lives in Iowa City.

Janet Thomas is an Australian who has been spending time in Iowa since 1987. During that time, she has married a pilot, raised a son, taught high school, danced, painted, and written some poems.

Tova Vitiello was born November 3, 1944 in Newark, New Jersey. She is a psychology professor emeritus and a retired psychotherapist. Her poems have been published in *Dana Review, Ain't I A Woman?, Windows of the Soul, Treasured Poems of America,* and *Sparrowgrass: Ten Years of Excellence.* Tova resides in Iowa City with her kayaks and camping gear.

Patricia Wellingham-Jones, Ph. D., R. N., is a Northern California writer, poet, editor, publisher, and three-time Pushcart Prize nominee in poetry. She is a former psychology researcher and lecturer in health and handwriting.

Editor Bios

Rustin Larson's poetry has appeared in *The New Yorker, The Iowa Review, North American Review, Poetry East, The Atlanta Review,* and other magazines. *Crazy Star* (Loess Hills Books, 2005) is his latest collection. A five-time Pushcart nominee, Rustin is also a graduate of the Vermont College M. F. A. in Writing. He was a featured Iowa Poet at the Des Moines National Poetry Festival in 2002 and 2004 and has been highlighted on the public radio programs *Live from Prairie Lights* and *Voices from the Prairie.*

Nynke Passi received her M. A. in creative writing from San Francisco State University. Her work has been published in many journals, including *Gulf Coast Review* and *The Anthology of New England Writers.* Her short story "The Kiss" was nominated for a Pushcart Prize in '96. She currently teaches creative writing and literature and is a member of the board of the New England Writers' Association.

Christine Schrum holds an M. A. in writing and is the Associate Editor of *The Iowa Source.* Her poetry has appeared in numerous anthologies and literary reviews, including *Poetry Motel, Collecting Moon Coins, The Dryland Fish, and Jellyfish.* She has co-judged several Blue Light Press poetry contests.

www.ingramcontent.com/pod-product-compliance
Lightning Source LLC
Chambersburg PA
CBHW031852090426
42741CB00005B/453